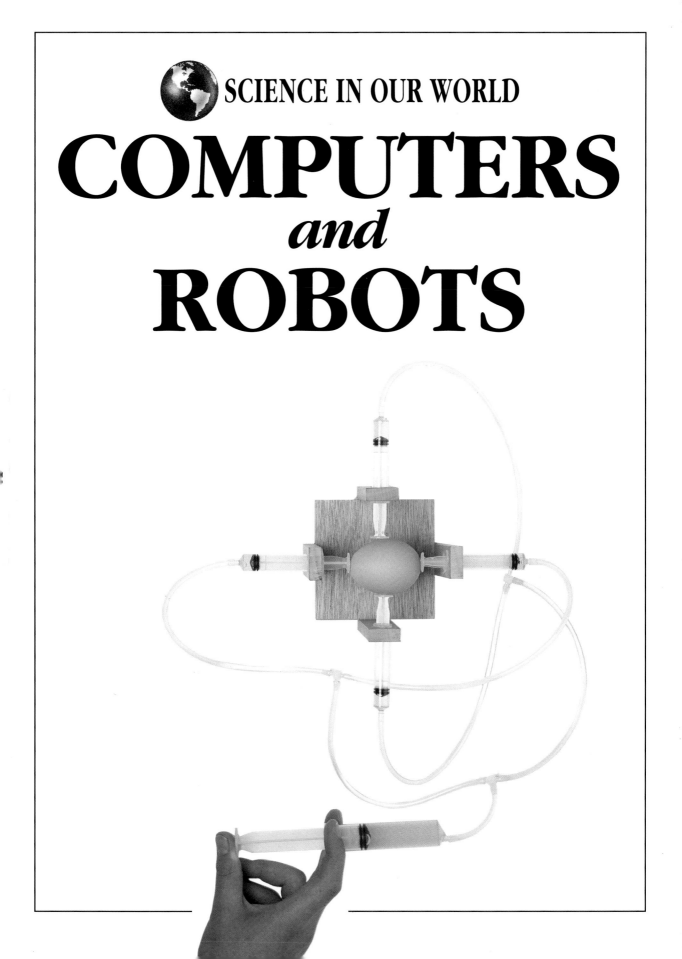

SCIENCE IN OUR WORLD

COMPUTERS
and
ROBOTS

Contributory Author
Brian Knapp, BSc, PhD
Art Director
Duncan McCrae, BSc
Special scientific models
*Tim Fulford, MA, Head of Design and Technology,
Leighton Park School*
Editorial consultants
Rita Owen, BSc and Sarah George, BEd
Special photography
Ian Gledhill
Illustrations
David Woodroffe
Science advisor
*Jack Brettle, BSc, PhD,
Chief Research Scientist, Pilkington plc*
Print consultants
Landmark Production Consultants Ltd
Printed and bound in Hong Kong
Produced by
EARTHSCAPE EDITIONS

First Published in the USA in 1994 by
GROLIER EDUCATIONAL CORPORATION
Sherman Turnpike, Danbury, CT 06816

Copyright © 1993
Atlantic Europe Publishing Company Limited

Library of Congress #93–078728

Cataloging information may be obtained directly
from Grolier Educational Corporation

ISBN 0–7172–7267–2

In this book you will find some words that have been shown in **bold** type. There is a full explanation of each of these words on pages 46 and 47.

On many pages you will find experiments that you might like to try for yourself. They have been put in a colored box like this.

Acknowledgments
The publishers would like to thank the following: Apple
Computer (UK) Ltd for their kind co-operation and advice,
Brother Industries Ltd (Japan), Fanuc Ltd (Japan), Japan
Foreign-Rights Centre (Japan), Leighton Park School,
National Westminster Bank Plc and Bert Price, Redlands
County Primary School and Sonning Common Garages Ltd.

Picture credits
t=top b=bottom l=left r=right
All photographs are from the Earthscape Editions library
except the following: Brother Industries Ltd *cover*, 35tr;
Canon (UK) Ltd, 29t, Fanuc Ltd 34tl, 34/35, 36bl.

Contents

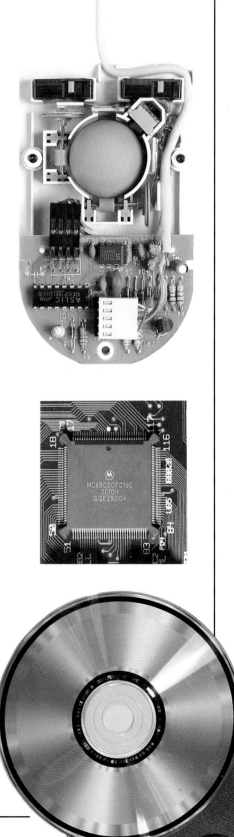

Introduction

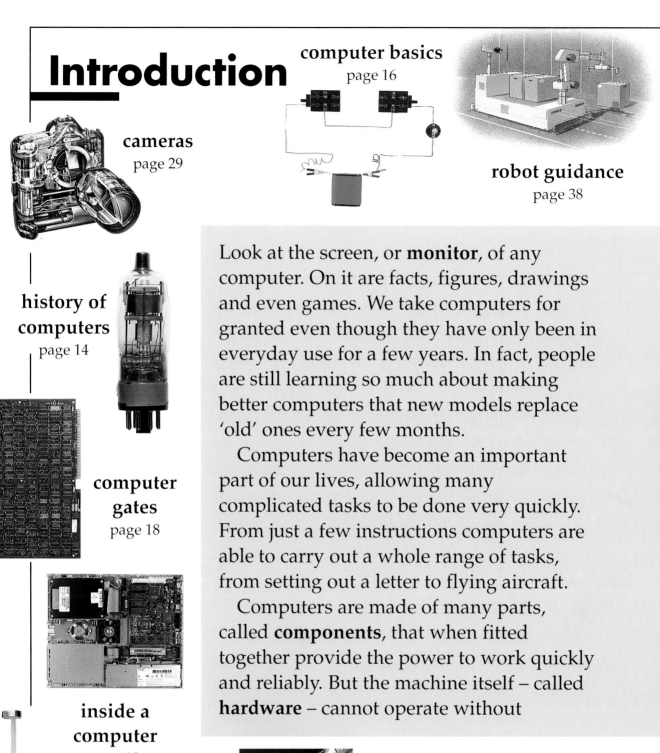

Look at the screen, or **monitor**, of any computer. On it are facts, figures, drawings and even games. We take computers for granted even though they have only been in everyday use for a few years. In fact, people are still learning so much about making better computers that new models replace 'old' ones every few months.

Computers have become an important part of our lives, allowing many complicated tasks to be done very quickly. From just a few instructions computers are able to carry out a whole range of tasks, from setting out a letter to flying aircraft.

Computers are made of many parts, called **components**, that when fitted together provide the power to work quickly and reliably. But the machine itself – called **hardware** – cannot operate without

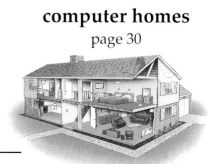

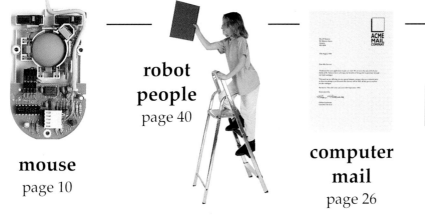

instructions – called **software** – and so while computer makers have been busy developing faster and faster parts, computer programmers – the people who write the instructions for the computers – have been equally busy using the latest techniques for finding shortcuts that will make the machines perform ever more complex tasks.

Many people are used to working with personal computers, known as PCs, which they keep at home or use in their offices or in their factories. But many computers are also used in everyday items such as telephones, washing machines and motor vehicles. Increasingly people have also coupled computers to machines, thereby producing robots.

Find out about the way computers and robots work as you read through this book. Just turn the page to begin your discoveries.

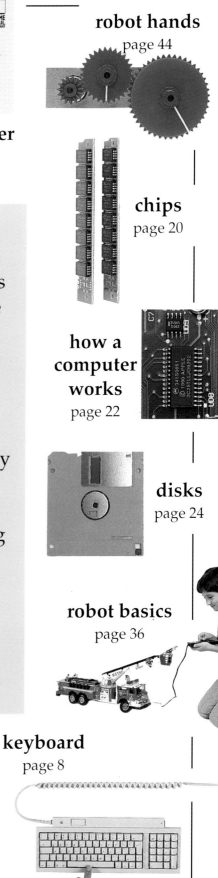

What is a computer?

The world's most complicated computer is inside your head – it is your brain. Although an electronic computer is vastly inferior to your brain, the way it works can best be described by comparing what goes on inside our heads with what happens inside a computer case.

1 The case for your brain is your skull. The case for the computer is a plastic box. Your brain communicates with the body and the outside world using ears, eyes, nose, mouth, a spinal cord and nerves. The computer communicates through electrical sockets, allowing keyboards, monitors and other devices to be plugged in.

2 Your brain learns about the outside world using your senses – a computer learns about the outside world through information from a keyboard, a mouse, disks and cables connected to other computers.

3 Your brain stores the information it has received in special cells; a computer stores information on disk and in special memory **chips**.

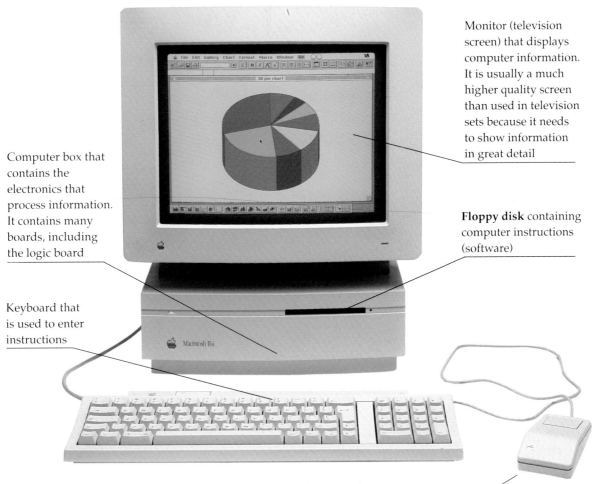

Monitor (television screen) that displays computer information. It is usually a much higher quality screen than used in television sets because it needs to show information in great detail

Computer box that contains the electronics that process information. It contains many boards, including the logic board

Floppy disk containing computer instructions (software)

Keyboard that is used to enter instructions

Mouse that is used to enter instructions and draw diagrams or move items about on the screen

4 Your brain is equipped from birth with certain basic instructions that keep you alive. For example, the brain sends instructions on breathing, keeping the heart beating and the lungs pumping. The computer has starting-up instructions imprinted inside its circuits so that when it is switched on (brought to life) it can start itself up.

5 Much of what the brain does is the result of learning through the use of language. The computer also learns from instructions; they are the programs fed into the machine by the operator.

6 The brain processes the information it has received and then issues instructions to the body. A computer processes the information on its logic board and then sends out instructions that can operate other computers, display patterns on a monitor or print on a printer.

Messages through the keyboard

Computers are usually fitted with a keyboard for typing instructions. Each key sends out a special **binary** code to the computer in patterns of 1s and 0s. Here are some examples of the codes and how they are used.

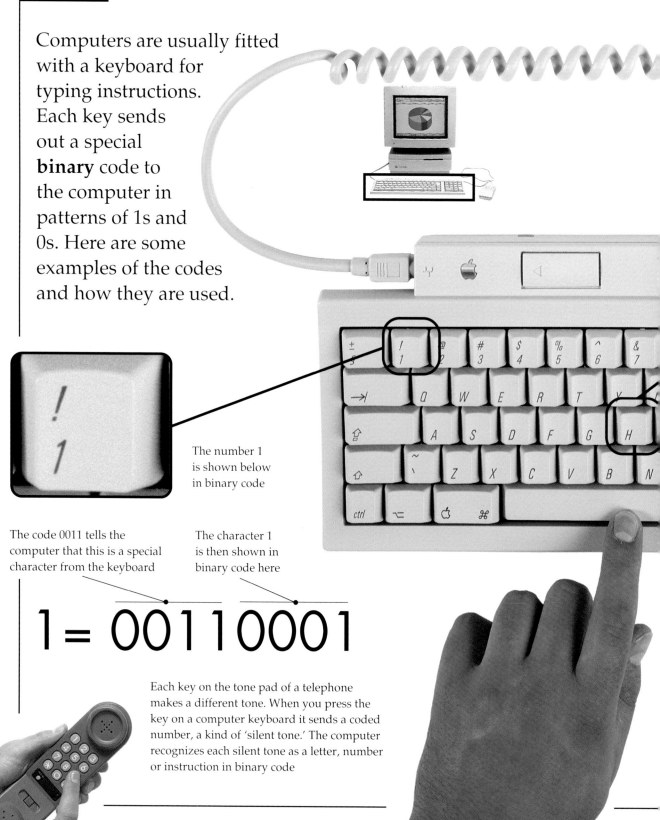

The number 1 is shown below in binary code

The code 0011 tells the computer that this is a special character from the keyboard

The character 1 is then shown in binary code here

1 = 00110001

Each key on the tone pad of a telephone makes a different tone. When you press the key on a computer keyboard it sends a coded number, a kind of 'silent tone.' The computer recognizes each silent tone as a letter, number or instruction in binary code

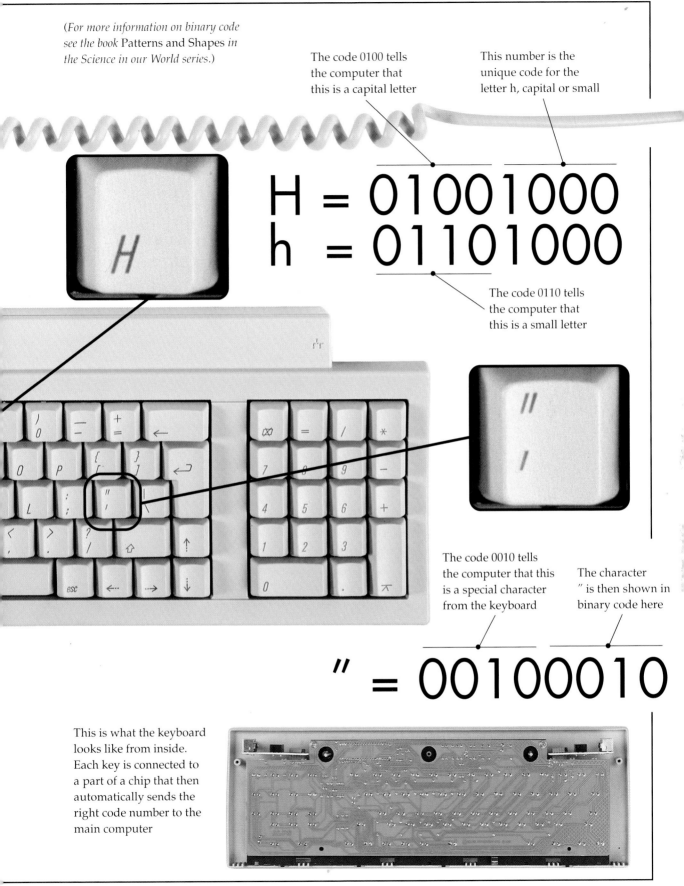

(For more information on binary code see the book Patterns and Shapes *in the Science in our World series.)*

The code 0100 tells the computer that this is a capital letter

This number is the unique code for the letter h, capital or small

$$H = 01001000$$
$$h = 01101000$$

The code 0110 tells the computer that this is a small letter

The code 0010 tells the computer that this is a special character from the keyboard

The character " is then shown in binary code here

$$" = 00100010$$

This is what the keyboard looks like from inside. Each key is connected to a part of a chip that then automatically sends the right code number to the main computer

9

Messages with a mouse

Many people use a keyboard to put information into a computer. But this is only one of several devices that can be used. One of the most common alternatives is known as a mouse.

How a mouse works
A mouse is the name given to small device usually connected to the computer by a cable. Moving the mouse moves a pointer on the monitor screen.

A mouse is designed to be pushed around a desktop and to fit comfortably inside the hand. It allows you to 'draw' instructions directly onto the monitor screen.

The mouse has a heavy rolling ball in its base. As it is pushed around, the ball, which is resting against the desktop, moves. The ball, in its turn, pushes against two small rollers that turn special wheels. The wheels send messages to the computer to tell it in which direction they are turning.

Buttons on top of the mouse allow the operator to tell the computer to do even more tasks.

Active buttons
An active button is a region on the monitor screen that can be used as a switch. Move the pointer to cover a button and then click the button on the mouse. This in turn clicks the active button on the screen, just as though you could press on the screen directly.

Experiment with a mouse and active buttons on your own computer.

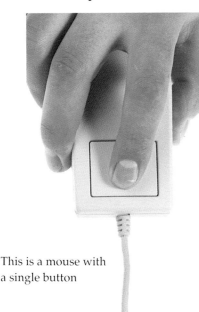

This is a mouse with a single button

Trackball

Removable cover

To make a mouse command work on the screen, move the mouse without pressing on the button. This causes the trackball to move and gives instructions to move the pointer on the screen. When you want the mouse to do something, you then click on a button or hold the button down

Inside a mouse

This is a common type of mouse used to operate personal computers. It is really a mini-computer that fits in the hand.

This cable connects the mouse to the computer

This is one of the disks that tells the computer about the side-to-side movements of the mouse. There is one with each roller

This is the trackball. Its weight holds it against the desktop as it moves

These rollers move when the trackball moves

This disk has contacts on its surface. It is like a moving switch. Changes in the way the switch moves tell the computer about forwards-backwards movement of the mouse

The messages from the rollers are passed through here and onto the circuit board at the back of the mouse

These are other components of the computer circuit

This is the chip of the 'on-board' processor. It reads the trackball movements and converts them into computer instructions

When you press the button on the top of the mouse these switch contacts close

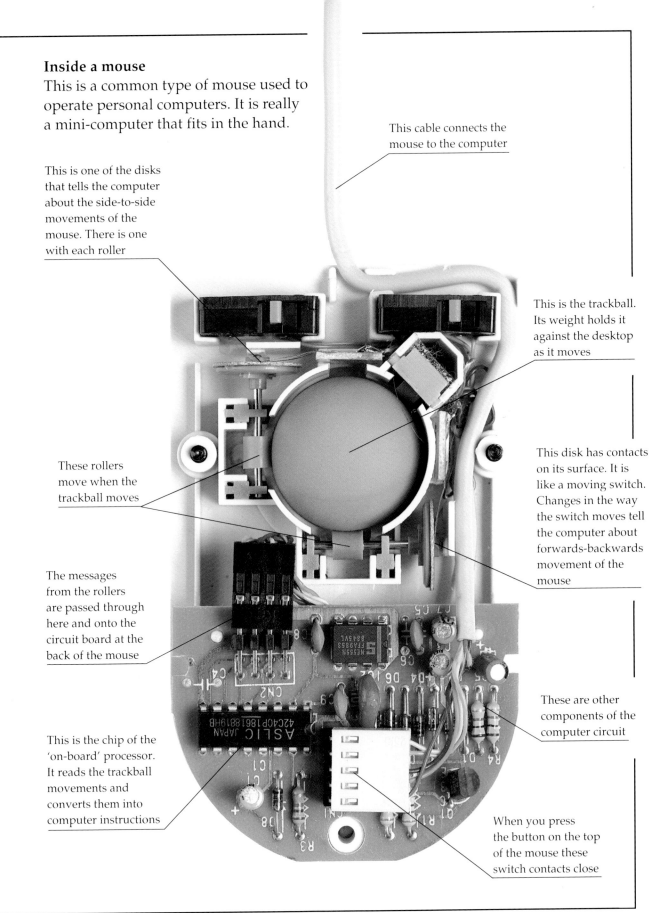

11

Inside the computer

Inside the computer box there is a printed circuit board that holds all the working components. It is called the logic board. Each part of the board has its own special function.

The computer must also be connected to many other external devices (called **peripherals**) if it is to work usefully. Here is a typical computer showing what the parts do.

Hard disk, able to store millions of bits of information (often over 100 million of them). It is much faster than a floppy disk

Loudspeaker for warning sounds, speech and music

FRONT

Floppy disk drive. Floppy disks are pushed into this case and read by a moving arm. Floppy disks store up to 2 million bits of information

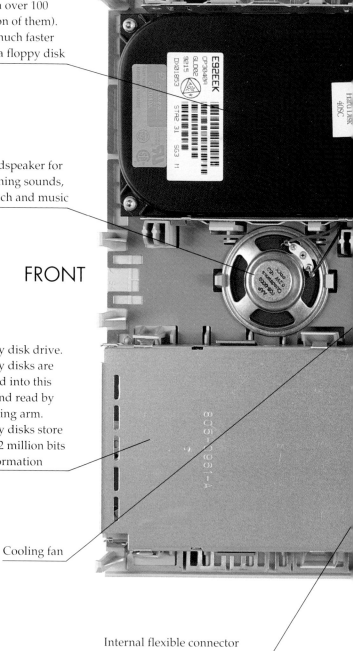

Cooling fan

Internal flexible connector joins different boards together.

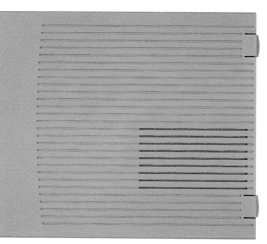

This is what the computer looks like with its cover on

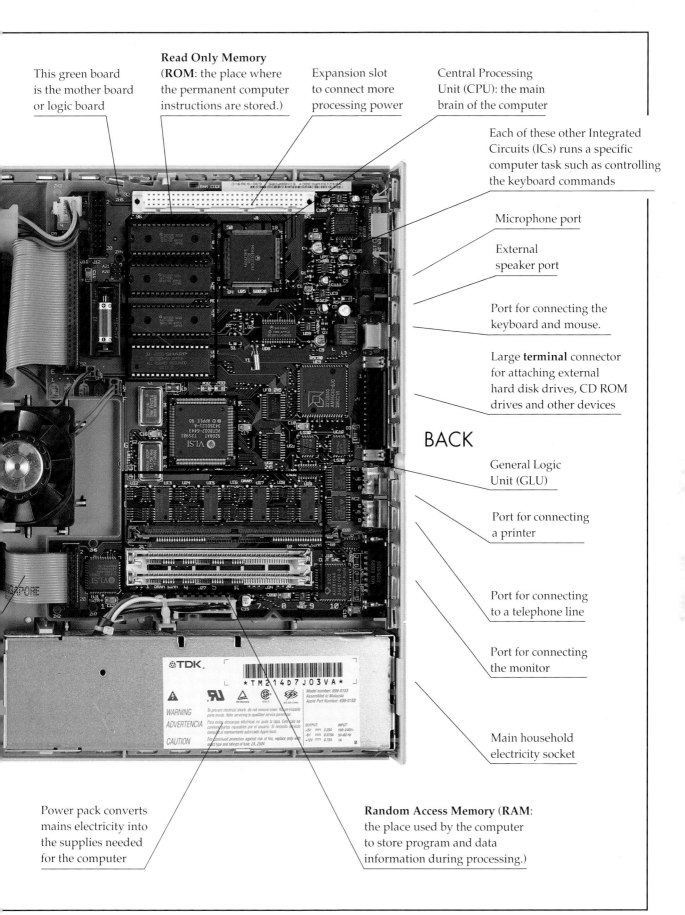

This green board is the mother board or logic board

Read Only Memory (**ROM**: the place where the permanent computer instructions are stored.)

Expansion slot to connect more processing power

Central Processing Unit (CPU): the main brain of the computer

Each of these other Integrated Circuits (ICs) runs a specific computer task such as controlling the keyboard commands

Microphone port

External speaker port

Port for connecting the keyboard and mouse.

Large **terminal** connector for attaching external hard disk drives, CD ROM drives and other devices

BACK

General Logic Unit (GLU)

Port for connecting a printer

Port for connecting to a telephone line

Port for connecting the monitor

Main household electricity socket

Power pack converts mains electricity into the supplies needed for the computer

Random Access Memory (**RAM**: the place used by the computer to store program and data information during processing.)

13

The heart of a computer

The 'heart' of a computer is the central processing unit (CPU). Although it can work extremely fast to process information, it is basically just a vast number of tiny switches arranged to work in special ways.

As new ways are found to make computers faster they can deal with ever more complex tasks. Here are some of the landmarks in discovery that have made modern computing possible.

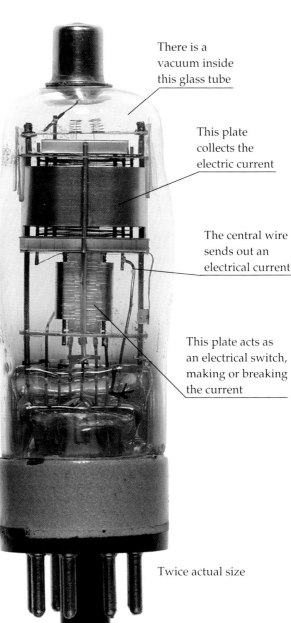

There is a vacuum inside this glass tube

This plate collects the electric current

The central wire sends out an electrical current

This plate acts as an electrical switch, making or breaking the current

Twice actual size

1 The mechanical switch

As the switch is flicked, a strip of springy metal is pushed down to connect one part of a circuit with another. This simple mechanical switch was invented over two centuries ago. Mechanical switches are still used in the home for switching on power supplies and lights.

2 The vacuum tube switch

An electronic valve, or **vacuum** tube, was invented about a century ago. Inside the tube are two or more metal plates and a wire that can be heated. When the wire is heated, by connecting it to an electrical supply, the vacuum tube can be used as a fast electrical switch. It is, however, bulky and it consumes a lot of electricity.

3 The transistor

About half a century ago the vacuum tube was replaced by pieces of material called **semi-conductors.** This change allowed electrical switches to be made smaller and to work without a heating element. This made the switches faster and used less power.

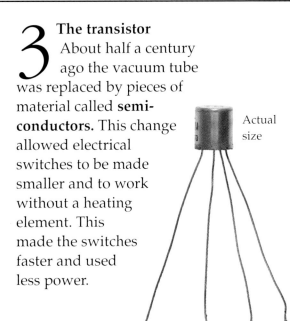

Actual size

4 The chip transistor

About a quarter of a century ago, it was discovered how to make the **transistor** part of a piece of an Integrated **Circuit**, or IC. This miniaturization allowed thousands of transistor switches to be built on just one tiny sliver of **silicon** and this is why it has become known as a silicon chip.

ICs work faster and are cheaper than single transistors and they are also much more reliable than other switches. Miniaturization of other components as well meant that entire circuits could be built into the same tiny chip.

Actual size

The IC shown here is encased in a block of plastic to make it big enough to handle. The number of wires connected to it hint at the enormous complexity that lies hidden inside

Enlarged

What computer switches do

The switches inside computer chips are often referred to as gates because messages can only pass along the computer system when these gates are open. The gates also stop messages inside the computer from getting mixed up and so allow the computer to do just one task at a time – very quickly.

Why simple switches are used
Computers can do some breathtaking things, and we rely on them to work at fast speed and to be right every time.

To be accurate and fast, a machine must not, in principle, be asked to do anything complicated. In fact, all computers are simply millions upon millions of tiny switches. The only thing they can be is on or off. This is why the **binary** code (1= on, 0 = off) is so vital to computer operations.

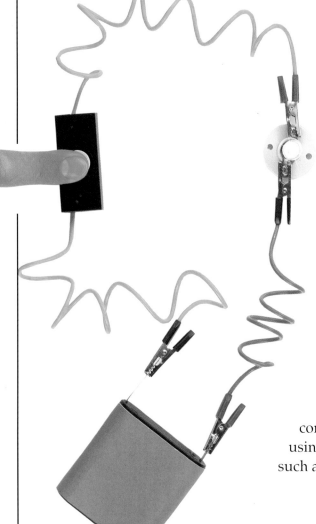

This is a simple mechanical switch. The current flows when the switch button is pressed and the bulb lights. So the push switch is a gate. It will only let a current flow when the strips of steel inside are connected

Three types of gate
Computers use three types of simple gate (see also page 18). The principle of the AND and OR gates are shown on the opposite page. The third type of switch is called a NOT gate. Its job is to prevent (NOT allow) a particular type of signal to pass. By clever programming, all computer processing can be done using combinations of simple switches such as those shown on these pages.

Using built logic boards

There are many commercial model logic boards that you can use to find out what computer gates can do. They allow sensors and gates to be connected in many ways. Devices as simple as this, when connected properly, control many household appliances, such as washing machines.

This is a typical logic board supplied by a commercial company. It gives much scope for experimenting with various gate combinations

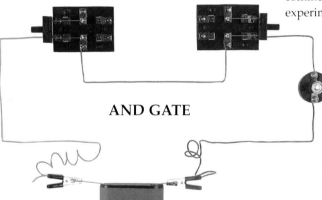

AND GATE

Making models of gates

The gates or switches in a modern computer are made of tiny electrical devices, so you cannot see them working. On this page there are some suggestions as to how you can find out what each type of switch does.

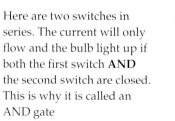

Here are two switches in series. The current will only flow and the bulb light up if both the first switch **AND** the second switch are closed. This is why it is called an AND gate

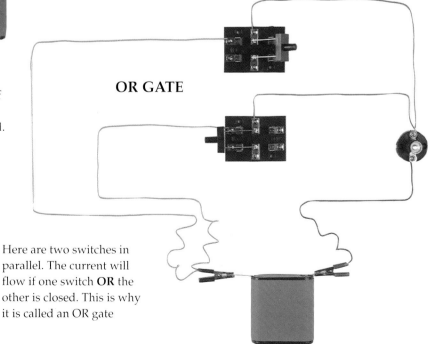

OR GATE

Here are two switches in parallel. The current will flow if one switch **OR** the other is closed. This is why it is called an OR gate

The power of computer gates

All computer messages can be processed using just three forms of computer gate – called AND, OR and NOT gates. On this page you can see a representation of how they are used to tell a computer to add 1 and 1 in binary language.

(For more information on binary code used in computers see the book Patterns and Shapes in the Science in our World *series.)*

Adding 1 and 1
The example on the opposite page shows how 1 + 1 are added using the three types of gate.
The keyboard instructions are:
Press 1+
The computer sends a message.
A signal is now sent along the wires to two gates. It passes through the right-hand (OR) gate but reaches the left-hand (AND) gate and waits.
Press 1=
Computer sends a second message along the same routes. The left gate has now received two signals (first AND second) and this allows a signal to pass through the AND gate.

Part of the signal proceeds to step up a counter and record a 1. The other part of the signal reaches a NOT gate and is stopped. This prevents two signals from reaching the right-hand AND gate and the counter to which it is connected remains at 0. The two counters now read 10.

When the calculation is complete the 10 in binary code will be converted by the computer circuits to show a character 2 on the monitor.

Computers use millions of gates to do all the calculations. Each chip can contain thousands of gates etched on its surface. The computer program controls how the signals arrive at each gate.

This picture shows just one part of a large (called 'mainframe') computer, such as would be used in many large offices; for example, in banks where millions of items are processed each day

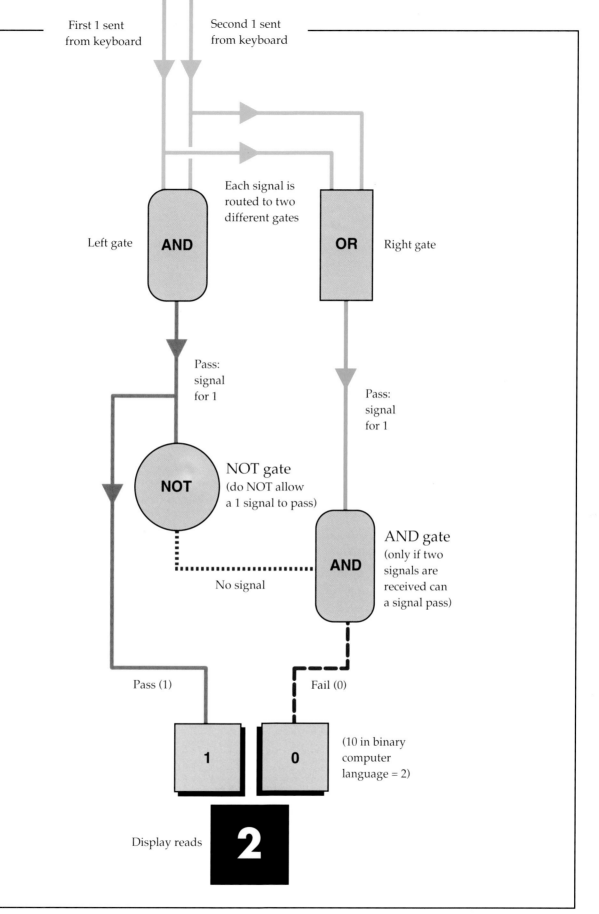

First 1 sent from keyboard

Second 1 sent from keyboard

Each signal is routed to two different gates

Left gate

AND

OR

Right gate

Pass: signal for 1

Pass: signal for 1

NOT gate (do NOT allow a 1 signal to pass)

NOT

AND

AND gate (only if two signals are received can a signal pass)

No signal

Pass (1)

Fail (0)

1

0

(10 in binary computer language = 2)

Display reads

2

Electronic chips

A chip is an Integrated Circuit (IC) that contains transistor switches and many other components in miniature form.

Just as our brains have certain regions for dealing with specific tasks, so the computer uses several types of chips, each dedicated to its own special task.

RAMs and ROMs

Computer memory chips are of two kinds: those that hold instructions permanently – called ROMs, Read Only Memory – and those that hold instructions and data only while the computer is working – called RAMs, Random Access Memory.

This is the logic board from a computer. Notice that it has many types of chips on it. How they work is shown on the next page

RAM is the learning brain of the computer. It is made up of banks of memory chips each placed on its own small circuit board.

The more of these the computer has, the more learning memory it has and the more easily a computer can do many tasks at the same time

ROM is etched onto the surface of the silicon layers inside these four ICs. They contain all the information to make the computer start up and wait for instructions and they also decide what kind of power the computer will have

This square-shaped chip is the main processor. It has a built-in clock on board

Paced by the clock

A computer has to perform its operations step by step; there would be chaos if millions of signals went around out of control. To make sure that each step is completed before another one is started, computers are controlled by an electronic clock that sends signals (electronic 'ticks') along the system.

Instructions and clock ticks each go through an AND gate, ensuring there is an instruction signal *and* a clock tick before the next action in the computer is made.

A computer clock 'ticks' millions of times a second, yet technologists are constantly trying to make circuits that change faster so that they can use faster clocks, which in turn will make computers work even more quickly.

21

How instructions move

When you press a key on the keyboard the computer instantly responds with a change on the monitor. Here is the complex route your instruction takes.

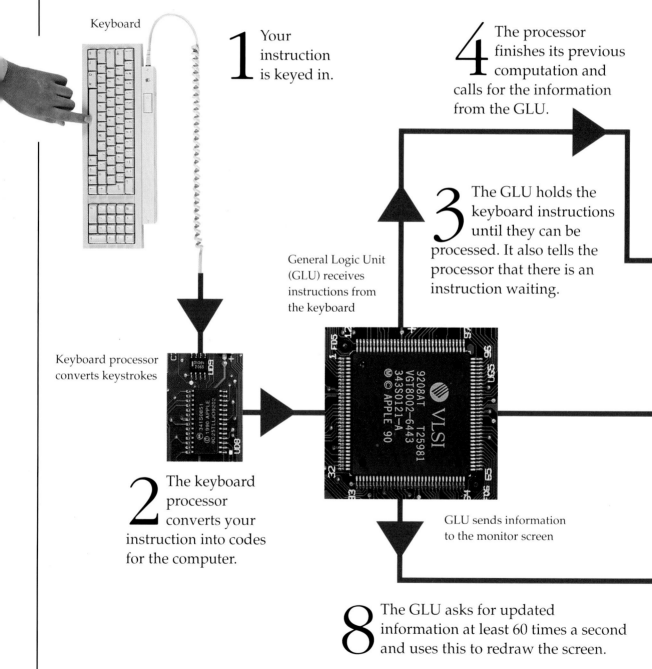

Keyboard

1 Your instruction is keyed in.

4 The processor finishes its previous computation and calls for the information from the GLU.

General Logic Unit (GLU) receives instructions from the keyboard

3 The GLU holds the keyboard instructions until they can be processed. It also tells the processor that there is an instruction waiting.

Keyboard processor converts keystrokes

VLSI
9208AT T25981
VGT8002-6443
343S0121-A
Ⓜ Ⓒ APPLE 90

2 The keyboard processor converts your instruction into codes for the computer.

GLU sends information to the monitor screen

8 The GLU asks for updated information at least 60 times a second and uses this to redraw the screen.

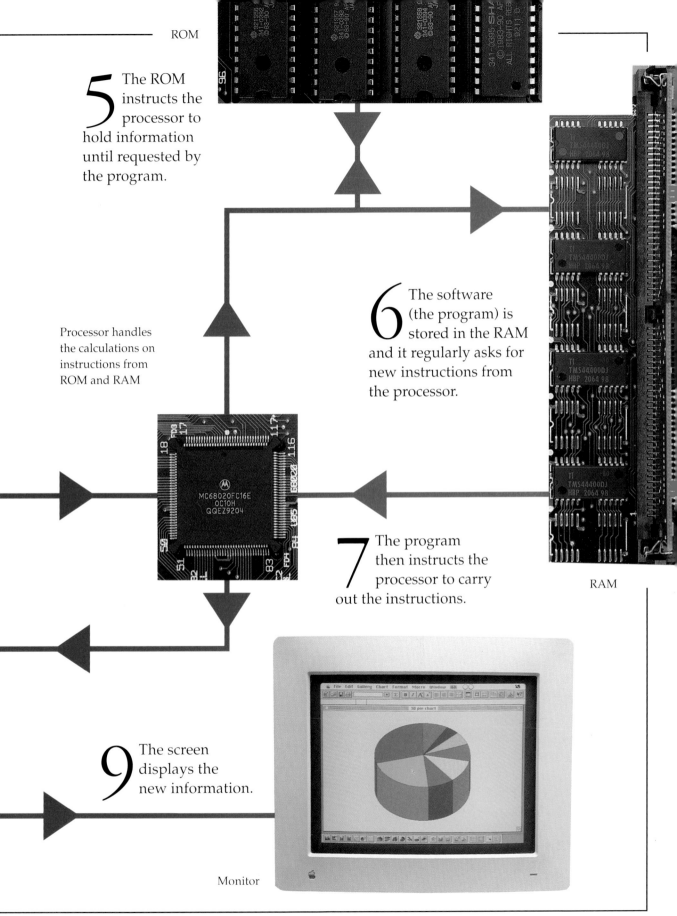

5 The ROM instructs the processor to hold information until requested by the program.

Processor handles the calculations on instructions from ROM and RAM

6 The software (the program) is stored in the RAM and it regularly asks for new instructions from the processor.

7 The program then instructs the processor to carry out the instructions.

RAM

9 The screen displays the new information.

Monitor

Storing information

There is not enough room inside chips to store very large amounts of information, and so most of the information that the computer needs – programs and data – are stored on disks.

The inside and outside of a floppy disk.

Storing information on disk

A disk is a flat circle of material with a special surface coating of magnetic particles.

There are two kinds of disks. One is a small portable disk called a floppy disk. It is made from plastic. This is a cheap way of storing relatively small amounts of information.

Floppy disks can only read or write slowly and they cannot contain much information. However, other disks – called hard disks – are bigger and can hold very large amounts of information that can be accessed more quickly.

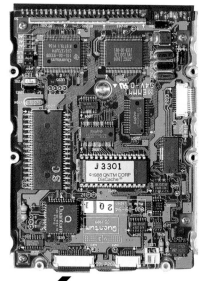

The picture below shows the inside of a hard disk.

The special heads sense the magnetism when reading or become magnetized when writing information

The head is moved across the disk by a precision motor called a stepper motor

There are two disks stacked on the same spindle. Stacking disks gives more storage space

The motor spins the disk

A hard disk accesses information very quickly. To manage all the tasks a separate mini-computer is attached to the hard disk case as shown in the picture above

How much memory?

Each keyboard key has its own number code made of 1s and 0s (see page 8). Each 1 or 0 is called a bit; every group of 8 bits is called a byte.

The amount of space available for storing the information is measured in bytes. A floppy disk often has space for between 400,000 and 2 million bytes of information (the equivalent of between 100 and 500 pages of typing). This is called a 2 Megabyte (MB) disk. Large disks, built into computers or separate boxes may store thousands of megabytes of information. Reels of magnetic tape can store even more.

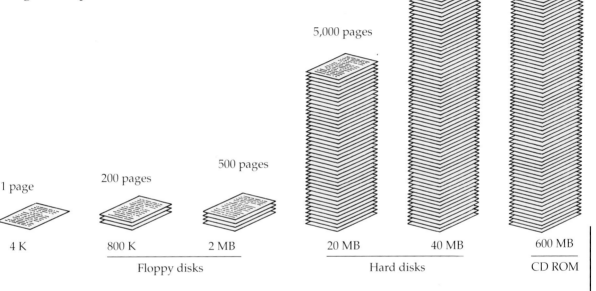

250,000 pages

10,000 pages

5,000 pages

500 pages

200 pages

1 page

4 K	800 K	2 MB	20 MB	40 MB	600 MB
	Floppy disks		Hard disks		CD ROM

CD ROM

This is a way of storing large amounts of information. It works just like a music CD player (and many CD ROM machines can play music CDs!). Information is held (in binary code) on the disc as a series of pits and laser light is used to read the pattern of pits.

CD ROM machines are used for storing very large amounts of information, such as the entire contents of an encyclopedia. More expensive machines can write data as well as read it.

A 600 MB CD ROM disc

Personal computer mail

Specialized computers – known as word processors – are used as electronic typewriters in offices throughout the world.

A word processor can make every letter look as though it was addressed and written individually even though it might simply be one of a huge batch. To do this, computer programmers devise programs that allow a list of names and addresses to be merged into a standard letter. When the merging is complete the letter is then printed. These are the steps that are involved.

The data disk holds the records of customers in magnetic form, as electronic record cards. Each part of each record card is given a reference (field) number. This allows the computer to select only those pieces of information that it needs to complete the letter

One information record may be:

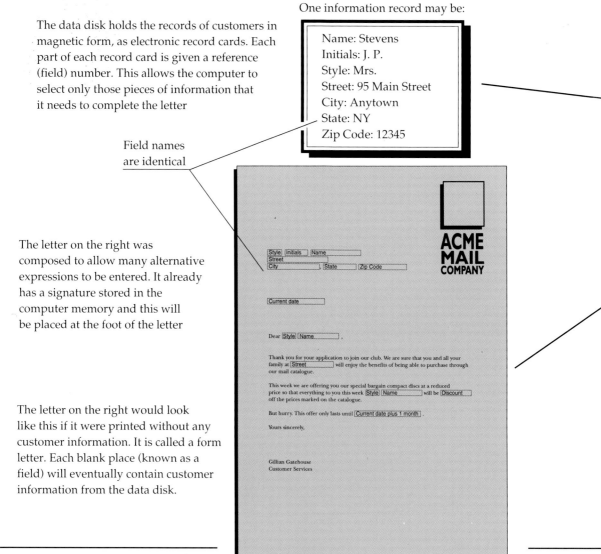

Name: Stevens
Initials: J. P.
Style: Mrs.
Street: 95 Main Street
City: Anytown
State: NY
Zip Code: 12345

Field names
are identical

The letter on the right was composed to allow many alternative expressions to be entered. It already has a signature stored in the computer memory and this will be placed at the foot of the letter

The letter on the right would look like this if it were printed without any customer information. It is called a form letter. Each blank place (known as a field) will eventually contain customer information from the data disk.

ACME
MAIL
COMPANY

Style Initials Name
Street
City , State Zip Code

Current date

Dear Style Name ,

Thank you for your application to join our club. We are sure that you and all your family at Street will enjoy the benefits of being able to purchase through our mail catalogue.

This week we are offering you our special bargain compact discs at a reduced price so that everything to you this week Style Name will be Discount off the prices marked on the catalogue.

But hurry. This offer only lasts until Current date plus 1 month .

Yours sincerely,

Gillian Gatehouse
Customer Services

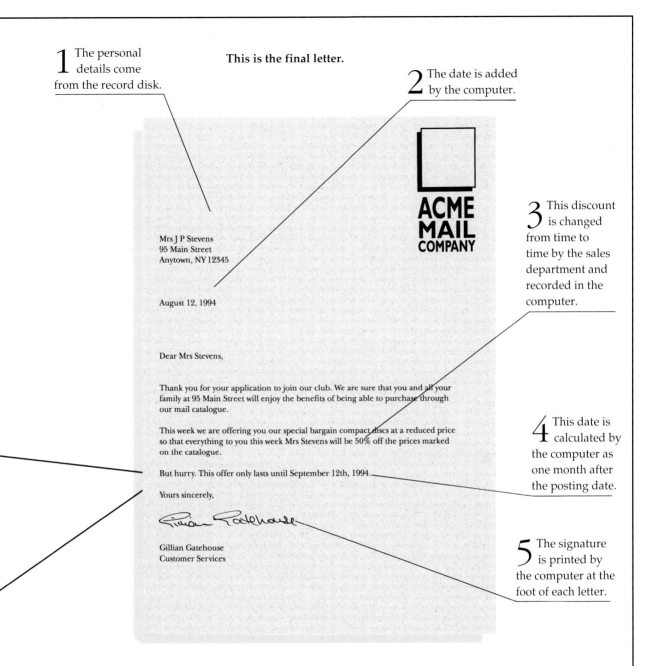

This is the final letter.

1 The personal details come from the record disk.

2 The date is added by the computer.

3 This discount is changed from time to time by the sales department and recorded in the computer.

4 This date is calculated by the computer as one month after the posting date.

5 The signature is printed by the computer at the foot of each letter.

Mrs J P Stevens
95 Main Street
Anytown, NY 12345

August 12, 1994

Dear Mrs Stevens,

Thank you for your application to join our club. We are sure that you and all your family at 95 Main Street will enjoy the benefits of being able to purchase through our mail catalogue.

This week we are offering you our special bargain compact discs at a reduced price so that everything to you this week Mrs Stevens will be 50% off the prices marked on the catalogue.

But hurry. This offer only lasts until September 12th, 1994.

Yours sincerely,

Gillian Gatehouse
Customer Services

Without human hand

As the computer begins its task it brings a new blank copy of the letter into its active memory. It also searches the disk for the next customer's record.

The computer then reads the letter and when it finds a blank field it examines the customer's records and inserts the correct words in the field.

When all the fields have been filled the computer then prints the letter (and the envelope) and an automatic machine folds the letter, puts it in the envelope, seals the envelope and adds a stamp. It is now ready for dispatch. No one has ever seen the letter, although the customer might think it was written specially for them. In reality it may have been just one of thousands.

Computers make things easier

Computers are used in so many ways today that we now take a lot of them for granted. Here are some common examples of how computers are being used.

Inside a modern automobile

Modern automobiles are very reliable. One reason for this is that moving parts have been replaced by computer chips wherever possible. For example, the spark needed to make the fuel burn is controlled by a computer and is always accurately timed.

Computers can sense and report possible problems. Computers are also able to make adjustments to give automatically the best possible fuel consumption.

The car radio is computer controlled. It uses electronic tuning to search for the strongest stations, to lock onto the strongest signal and then keep the signal free from distortion

Computers receive information about road conditions from transmitting stations placed along highways or direct from satellites. This allows people to avoid traffic jams

The engine control system monitors the speed of the engine, the rate the fuel gets to the cylinders and the altitude of the vehicle and then adjusts the sparking and fuel to give the most efficient use of fuel

Sensors are placed around the car to feed information to the central processing unit

Sensors in the wheels tell the computer when the brakes are about to lock and cause a skid. The brakes are released just enough to stop this from happening (a system called ABS)

The exposure and lens opening (aperture) are automatically calculated and the camera adjusted, all while the button is being pressed to take a shot

The computer displays information on this panel and also inside the viewfinder

The type of film is automatically detected and the correct programs chosen to match it

This is the logic board for the camera computer

Chip inside the lens directs the motor until the lens is in focus

The computer counts the shots and automatically advances the film, then rewinds at the end

The computer senses the battery and warns of low power

The computer can tell the motorist how much fuel he is using and help him to drive in a style that is more efficient; it can also remember the average speed he has been driving at and tell him when he is likely to arrive at his destination.

Inside a modern camera

Modern cameras make successful photography much easier by using tiny computers tucked away inside the case.

When you begin to press down on the button, the computer snaps into action. It begins to assess the picture, turning the lens until the subject is in focus. Using information from photoelectric cells placed on the viewing mirror, the computer can compare the subject with thousands of stored images and choose the best shutter speed and lens opening.

This all happens so quickly while the button is being pressed down that you notice no apparent delay.

As soon as the photograph has been taken the camera winds the film. It can also count to the end of the film, rewind automatically and monitor the battery power.

Computers around us

You may think your home computer is the one sitting on your bedroom table, but there are many more around the home and in the street nearby than you might at first realize.

Home computers are used for playing games, writing letters, business and connecting to an electronic mail box

In the kitchen the toaster, the oven, the washing machine and the dishwasher may all be controlled in their programmed cycles by computers

This **controller** box is a computer that monitors all the burglar devices

Banking cards

Many people now have banking cards. These small pieces of plastic allow things to be bought without the need to carry large amounts of money about.

If someone wants to get money from a cash machine they must first insert their plastic card into the machine and then enter their personal number using a keyboard. A computer then checks the information on the card's magnetic stripe, checks the customer's records and pays the money.

Telephones were early users of computers because electronic switching is faster and more reliable than mechanical versions. Modern phones can answer and record calls automatically, store telephone numbers in memory and answer with messages or transfer calls if you are out.

Modern phones can also automatically find the cheapest route for your call. Several telephones can be connected together as an intercom or extensions provided for a smoke detector and a burglar alarm

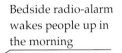

Bedside radio-alarm wakes people up in the morning

This is a movement detector. The computer senses movement by the heat radiated by hot engines, people and animals. It can switch on alarms or a welcome light

An electronic diary will record thousands of entries as well as alert you to appointments that need to be kept

Televisions and music centers are controlled by computers. They contain chips to receive signals, to keep the signal tuned in, to receive text data, to store pictures and to operate a remote control

What is a robot?

A robot is a machine that can perform a number of tasks involving some kind of movement. A robot is a very sophisticated piece of automatic machinery, driven by instructions from a complex computer program. The difference between an **automated** machine and a robot is that the robot can feed back information allowing the computer to make corrections or adjustments.

How robots work

1 Computer sends instructions to the machine.

2 Robot arm, leg, hand moves according to the computer directions.

3 Robot senses what it has done.

4 Robot feeds back completed effect of action to computer so that new instructions can be issued.

Robot value
Robots can be driven by motors, liquids or gases (see the following pages). They can swivel very quickly and they can move an 'arm' and a 'hand' both quickly and accurately and they can therefore be used for **precision** work.

Other examples of how robots are commonly used are shown on the following pages.

Robots are used extensively in space because they can work well in weightless, airless conditions where people have to wear clumsy protective clothing. These photographs show the way robots are used to manipulate satellites for launch or recovery from the cargo bay of a space shuttle and (inset picture) how they also can be used to assist in complicated repairs.

Space robots can be less bulky than their Earth-bound counterparts because the objects they manipulate are weightless and easy to move.

Robots in our world

Robots are useful for performing accurate repetitive tasks in factories because they can be programmed to work very quickly and accurately. For example, they can spot weld pieces of a vehicle chassis or fit components into an electronic circuit

board speedily and without tiring.

Robots can also be used in dangerous environments such as when dealing with hot, dusty or radioactive material in the depths of the oceans or in space.

Robots assembling electronic products. The robot performs complex and repetitive tasks very quickly

Principles of robotics

Designers have to build robots to make the best use of the materials available. For this reason robots are rarely designed to look like people.

Robots are most efficient, and cost less to construct, when each one is designed to do a limited range of tasks. For this reason a sequence of tasks is best performed by a sequence of robots each doing a part of the overall job.

This factory production line consists of rows of robots whose task is to make new robots!

Robots will spray paint evenly, giving each item an even and identical finish. Paint sprays may also cause health risks; the use of robots reduces the need for people to work in such a hazardous environment

Robotic brain

Robots are controlled by instructions from their computer brain. Many robot tasks are so complicated that they use huge amounts of computer power. This is one reason that the use of robots increases in line with faster, smaller and more powerful computers.

Some computers now have the ability to 'learn' the required movements during a special guidance session. On this first 'learning' occasion a human operator moves the robot through its normal routine and the computer memorizes the moves; thereafter the robot can copy this sequence of moves exactly.

Robot basics

The joints and muscles on a human body are so well developed that, for example, limbs can be moved freely in almost every direction. Robots have much simpler joints, with limbs controlled by motors or pistons.

In fact, it is almost impossible to copy the way a human joint work; robot designers have to solve the problem of movement in a very different way.

Complete movement

Three motors are needed to give complete movement in all dimensions.

The fire engine toy shown below achieves many movements by the use of several motors, each of which performs just a simple movement.

Pressing combinations of the control buttons at the same time allows complete movement of the robot arm (fire ladder) as well as the robot body (fire engine). A programmer's task would be to program the sequence of button pressing.

This is the remote control panel for the fire engine. A robot needs a separate instruction for each movement. When no buttons are pressed the instruction is 'do nothing'

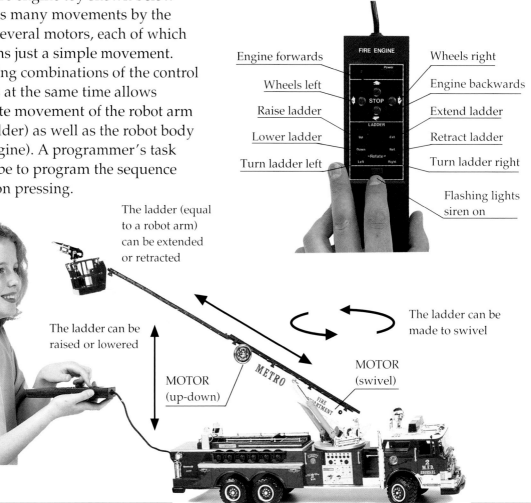

FIRE ENGINE

Engine forwards

Wheels left

Raise ladder

Lower ladder

Turn ladder left

Wheels right

Engine backwards

Extend ladder

Retract ladder

Turn ladder right

Flashing lights siren on

The ladder (equal to a robot arm) can be extended or retracted

The ladder can be raised or lowered

The ladder can be made to swivel

MOTOR (up-down)

MOTOR (swivel)

Investigate robot design

The **remote control** device shown above combines two tasks
that could be operated by a single motor: it will move away
from the operator while closing on an object.

Make a model grabber for yourself using card and envelope
pins and find out about some of the problems of operating it.
Is it easy to 'feel' how hard you are holding the object? Is it
easy to move the arm and pick up the object?

Now try operating a robot toy like the one shown opposite.
Find out if it is easier to control when each kind of movement
is activated by a separate button.

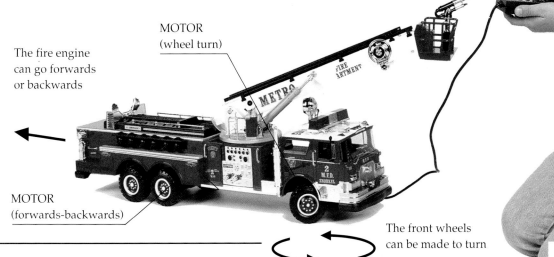

MOTOR
(wheel turn)

The fire engine
can go forwards
or backwards

MOTOR
(forwards-backwards)

The front wheels
can be made to turn

37

Sensing the environment

A moving robot must have many on-board sensors so that it can tell what its environment is like. For example, it must avoid crashing into other robots, its surroundings or people; it must not go too near to heat sources or up slopes that would cause it to fall over; and it must find its way about. All of these requirements need sensors, some of which are shown here.

Lenses can focus automatically. As the lens adjusts to stay in focus, so the distance information is sent to the computer to tell it how far the nearest obstacle is

Antenna for communicating with other computers

Video cameras enable human operators to work the robot by remote control

If you are in the dark you feel your way around your environment. As soon as your hands touch something a signal is sent to your brain.

A robot is always 'in the dark' and the simplest way to give it sensing hands is to fit antennae. At the base of each **antenna** is an object called a **transducer**. If the antenna touches something, the transducer sends a signal to the computer so that corrections can be made to the course

Transducer in base of antenna

On-board computer

This robot moves motor parts around a warehouse. It uses many of the features shown in the main picture on these pages

Keeping upright

It is important that moving robots do not fall over. One way to do this is to use a small device for sensing the vertical. Some robots use gyroscopes, others use a pendulum inside the robot. Because gravity always keeps the pendulum vertical, if the robot starts to tilt, a sensor on the pendulum will operate, completing a circuit. The robot will then stop.

Control arm

A beam of laser light is bounced off the surroundings and the time for its return measured to find out the distance to the nearest obstacle

Very high pitched (ultrasonic) sound waves are bounced off the object ahead and analyzed by the computer to sense how fast the robot is approaching an obstacle

Infrared sensors tell a robot that a moving object is near or that it is moving too close to a source of heat

A robot can be made to follow a metal band laid down on a road. Under the robot is a sensor that detects the metal and makes it part of its electronic circuit. If the robot starts to wander from the metal track, the electronics are disturbed and the computer instructs the steering motors to turn the wheels to bring it back on course

Copying humans

Robots are normally designed to perform their tasks most efficiently, and as a result they rarely look like people. However, scientists continue to be interested in robots that are the same general shape as humans because robots would then be able to do the jobs humans naturally do: robot and human would be interchangeable and activities suited to people would also be directly suitable for robots. The task of making a robot that behaves like a person is formidable. Here are some of the problems to be overcome.

1 The need for balance
A person uses special parts of the inner ear to keep their balance; the brain constantly 'tweaks' the muscles to keep the body from falling over.

2 The need to be mobile
Legs provide people with a ready means of moving across uneven ground, climbing steps, jumping over gaps and supporting bodies.

Fluid levels in the inner ear are used for balance.

3 The need for variable reach
A person's arm can be moved into a large number of positions, extended, drawn in and turned in its socket. An arm is also incredibly powerful for its weight and size.

4 The need to be dextrous

Dextrous means to be able to hold small objects, to fit them together and otherwise do delicate tasks. Our fingers and thumbs are very sensitive to pressure, they can move in many directions and they can also grip very firmly.

Hands

Hands have more joints in them than almost any other part of the body. This is what allows them to move so freely.

Each joint is surrounded by two sets of muscles. Feel the fingers of your hands and discover the positions of the muscles surrounding each joint. These slim-line muscles, together with the use of the thumb, are the key to accurate and skillful holding.

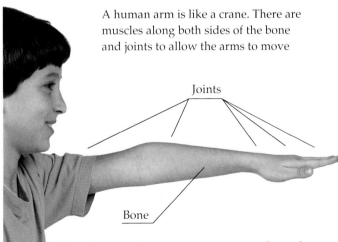

A human arm is like a crane. There are muscles along both sides of the bone and joints to allow the arms to move

Joints

Bone

Muscles can only contract, so two sets of muscles are needed, one on either side of the joint

The state of progress

On these pages are the four main areas that science and technology have to overcome if they are to make a working human-shape robot. Because it is relatively easy to make joints work, robotic arms and hands have been widely built and used. By contrast, it is extremely difficult for a two-legged robot to remain balanced. To keep in balance a robot would need all the computing power of a modern supercomputer. Such computers are not portable, making walking robots unlikely for many years to come.

Pressure joints

It is quite easy to make flexible joints by applying pressure to a gas or a liquid in a tube. The pressure is then sent down the tube to operate a mechanism. This system, used in automobile brakes, for example, is very reliable. You can see how it works here and how it might be used in robots.

Cylinders and pistons using the principles shown in these models are used for moving heavy loads; electric motors are used where extreme precision is needed.

3 The plunger piston is pushed up and the weight rises.

⚠️
Caution
Use special non-medical syringes for these experiments

2 Fluid is pushed up through the tube.

1 The fingers push the lower plunger

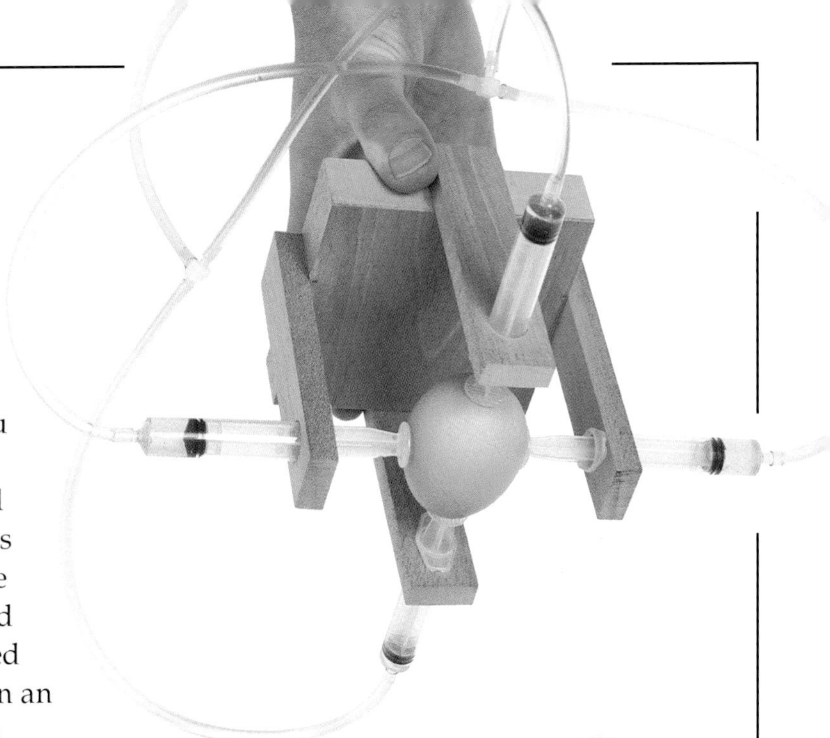

Investigate fluid control

A fluid is a liquid or a gas. Both can be used to control a movement at a remote location.

To show how this works you need two small syringes and a length of flexible pipe that will fit tightly over the syringe ends as shown in the pictures on the opposite page. Fill the tube and one of the syringes with colored liquid. Fix the empty syringe in an upright position and balance a weight on the plunger. Squeeze the free plunger and watch the weight lift. You have made a remote (robotic) control.

Use five syringes and join the tubes with T-pieces (from a science equipment supplier) as shown on the right. They can be fixed so that when one is pushed the other four grip an egg, just like a robot hand. Can you make the model shown on the left and find out about robot gripping power? Can you build the egg gripper shown above? Can you apply enough pressure to crush the egg?

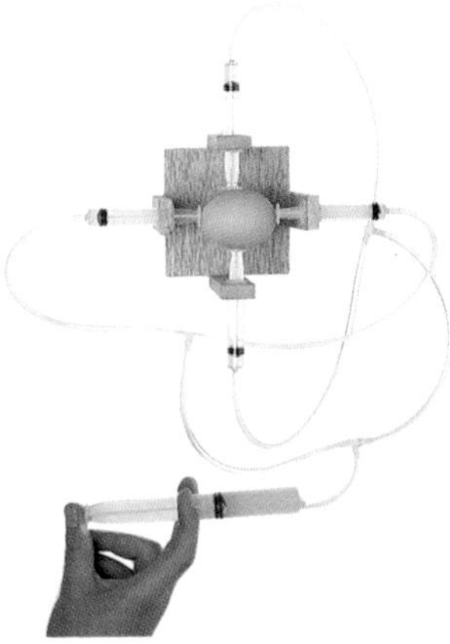

This toy backhoe uses air-driven (pneumatic) cylinders and pistons to operate the arm and the digger. Switches to operate it are at the back. The plunger attached to the piston for filling the circuits with air is in the middle

43

Making robot hands

Many robots use motors to move their arms and hands. A small electric motor can be made to move very precisely if it is connected through gear wheels, wires or rods. Here are some ways to make motors move things with accuracy.

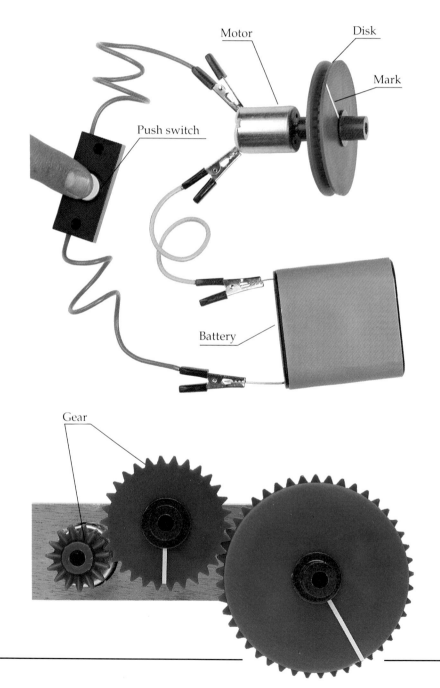

1 Connect a small electric motor to a battery and push switch, as shown here. Fit a wheel to the motor and mark the edge of the disk so that you can see how far the wheel has moved.

Motor

Disk

Mark

Push switch

Battery

2 Push the switch and watch the wheel turn. See how closely you can control where the disk will stop.

3 Because the disk is connected directly to the motor it is difficult to control. But if a gear is added, the fast spinning motor will turn the wheel only slowly. Add a gear and test that you now have more control over the wheel.

Gear

This flexible tube operates a grab hand simply by pushing down on the plunger. When the plunger is released the grab closes and grips the object, allowing it to be carried. This is a very simple mechanical robot hand

Make a robot hand

Try to make your own moving finger using simple constructional materials, such as those shown below. The size of the motor wheel controls the speed at which the finger moves. Experiment with different gears to see which gives good control over the movement of the finger. Can you work out a way of preventing the finger from gripping too tightly?

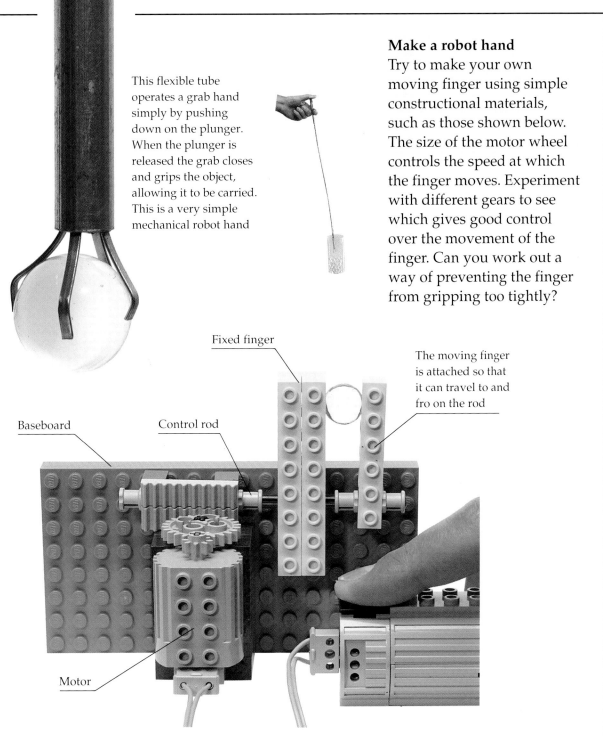

Fixed finger

The moving finger is attached so that it can travel to and fro on the rod

Baseboard

Control rod

Motor

Making to and fro motion

A motor can be used to make a machine turn, but it can also be used to make it go backwards and forwards.

Turning movements are converted into backwards and forwards movement through gears and rods.

New words

antenna

a rod-like sensing device. In the case of a robot an antenna may give important information about the environment it touches

automatic/automated

referring to a machine that works automatically and is able to perform a certain task independently. An automated system is one in which a set of machines do a number of tasks automatically, one perhaps feeding material to another

binary

the system of numbers that uses only combinations of 1 and 0 to describe all numbers. In this system, for example, the combination 10 (1 and 0) is 2. This system is particularly important in computing because 1 can be represented as a switch set to 'on' and 0 can be represented by a switch set to 'off'

chip

the general term to describe an integrated circuit etched onto the surface of a thin piece of silicon

circuit

a network of electrical components and connections. Circuits are built to perform special tasks and one circuit is often used linked to many others

component

a component is a small part of a more complex object. Electrical components include resistors, capacitors and chips; mechanical components include gears, rods and pivots

controller

a device that enables an operator to control a robot or other automated equipment. The controller is often a set of switches that control each movement of a robot

floppy disk

a small disk used to store magnetic information for a computer

hard disk

a disk made from aluminum and coated with magnetic material

hardware

in computing terms the hardware comprises all the physical parts of a computer such as the keyboard, the monitor, the computer processing unit and the printer

monitor

the display unit for a computer. The monitor display usually looks like a television screen

peripheral
any piece of computer hardware that is not part of the central computer 'box.' Keyboards, monitors and printers are all peripherals

precision
a high degree of exactness and accuracy

remote control
most machines are directly controlled by people. Their hands touch the switches on the machine or move wheels, levers, etc. If the controlling is achieved through a cable or by radio then it is said to be under remote control

semiconductor
a substance such as silicon that can conduct electricity usually because impurities have been added in a special way. The word is also used to describe a device such as a transistor that depends on the properties of semiconductor material

silicon
this is a basic substance, or element, of the Universe like lead or oxygen. It is usually found as a component of sand. In its pure form it is a gray solid

software
the name given to any computer instruction, usually a program

terminal
a connector, or socket, fixed to a piece of equipment that allows a cable to be connected to it; in computer usage the word *port* can be used to mean 'terminal'. It is also the name given to a computer keyboard and monitor that are linked to a main networked computer and that allows many people access to the same large computer processing power

transducer
a device that changes, for example, a pressure into an electrical signal. Transducers are useful in robotics because they enable a robot to develop a sense of touch

transistor
a small device made of semi-conductor material and that can work as a tiny switch or to make an electrical signal stronger. Thousands of transistors can be placed inside a chip, saving space and materials. Transistors are the basic building blocks of a computer system

vacuum
when air has been completely pumped out of a vessel, the absence of material inside is called a vacuum. A true vacuum is almost impossible to achieve, and so it is common to use the word *vacuum* to describe a space that has had most of the air pumped out of it

Index